THE·BESOM·MAKER

&

OTHER·COVNTRY·FOLK·SONGS

Collected and Illustrated

by HEYWOOD·SVMNER

1888.

Folk Music

Folk music includes both traditional music and the genre that evolved from it during the twentieth century folk revival. Traditional folk music has been broadly defined as music transmitted orally, without a single 'composer', as contrasted with commercial and classical styles.

A consistent and all-encompassing definition of traditional folk music is elusive however. The terms *folk music*, *folk song*, and *folk dance* are comparatively recent expressions. They are extensions of the term *folklore*, which was coined in 1846 by the English antiquarian William Thoms to describe 'the traditions, customs, and superstitions of the uncultured classes.' The term is further derived from the German expression *Volk*, in the sense of 'the people as a whole' as applied to popular and national music by Johann Gottfried Herder and the German Romantics over half a century earlier. The emergence of the term 'folk' coincided with the mid-nineteenth century outburst of national feeling all over Europe, particularly at the edges of Europe, where national identity was most strongly asserted.

Folk music may tend to have certain characteristics but it cannot clearly be differentiated in purely musical terms. One meaning often given is that of 'old songs, with no known composers', another is that of music that has been submitted to an evolutionary 'process of oral transmission.... the fashioning and re-fashioning of the music by the community that give it its folk character.' For scholars such as Béla Bartók, (a Hungarian composer and pianist who collected and studied folk music – as one of the founders of comparative musicology and ethnomusicology) there was a sense of the music of the country as distinct from that of the town. Folk music was seen as the authentic expression of a way of life now past or about to disappear, particularly in a community uninfluenced by modern 'artistic' and commercial music.

Throughout most of human prehistory and history, listening to recorded music was not possible. Music was made by common people during both their work and leisure. The work of economic production was often manual and communal. Manual labour often included singing by the workers, which served several practical purposes. It reduced the boredom of repetitive tasks, it kept the rhythm during synchronized pushes and pulls, and it set the pace of many activities such as planting, weeding, reaping, threshing, weaving, and milling. In leisure time, singing and playing musical instruments were common forms of entertainment and history-telling – even more common than today, when electrically enabled technologies made these forms of information-sharing competitive.

Opinions differ greatly on the origins of folk music. Some said it was art music that was changed and probably debased by oral transmission – others said it reflects the character of the race that produced it. 'Individual' and 'Collective' theories of its dissemination abound. Traditionally, the cultural transmission of folk music is through learning by ear, although notation may also be used, and traditional cultures that did not rely on written music produced work that was exceedingly difficult to categorise.

Despite this, many scholars attempted just such an endeavour, and the English term 'folklore', entered the vocabulary of many continental European nations, each of which had its folk-song collectors and revivalists.

Cecil Sharp (the founding father of the folklore revival in England in the early twentieth century) had an influential idea about the process of folk variation: he felt that the competing variants of a traditional song would undergo a process akin to biological natural selection: only those new variants that were the most appealing to ordinary singers would be picked up by others and transmitted onward in time. Thus, over time we would expect each traditional song to become aesthetically ever more appealing — it would be collectively composed to perfection, as it were, by the community.

The distinction between 'authentic' folk and national and popular song in general has always been loose. The International Folk Music Council definition allows that the term can also apply to music that 'has originated with an individual composer and has subsequently been absorbed into the unwritten, living tradition of a community.' But the term does not cover a song, dance, or tune that has been taken over ready-made and remains unchanged. Apart from instrumental music that forms a part of traditional folk music, especially dance music traditions, much traditional folk music is vocal music, since the instrument that makes such music is usually handy. As such, most traditional folk music has meaningful, historically significant lyrics.

Narrative verse looms large in the traditional folk music of many cultures. This encompasses such forms as traditional epic poetry, much of which was meant originally for oral performance, sometimes accompanied by instruments. Many epic poems of various cultures were pieced together from shorter pieces of traditional narrative verse, which explains their episodic structure and often their *in medias res* plot developments. Other forms of traditional narrative verse (and hence folkloric singing) relate the outcomes of battles and other tragedies or natural disasters. Sometimes, as in the triumphant *Song of Deborah* found in the Biblical *Book of Judges*, these songs celebrate victory. Laments for lost battles and wars, and the lives lost in them, are equally prominent in many traditions; these laments keeping alive the cause for which the battle was fought.

Hymns and other forms of religious music are often of traditional and unknown origin, though their inclusion in the folkloric canon is debatable. Western musical notation was originally created to preserve the lines of Gregorian chant, which before its invention was taught as an oral tradition in monastic communities. Traditional songs such as *Green grow the rushes* (originating in the nineteenth century) present religious lore in a mnemonic form. In the Western world, Christmas carols and other traditional songs also preserve religious lore in song form. Other common forms of folk signing include work songs with 'call and response' structures, designed to coordinate labourer's efforts. Often arising in the terrible times of slavery and forced labour, they were frequently, but not invariably composed by the community that sung them. In the American armed forces, a lively tradition of jody calls

('Duckworth chants') are sung while soldiers are on the march, and all over the world, professional sailors make great use of sea shanties. Nursery rhymes, love poetry and nonsense verse also are also frequent subjects of traditional folk songs.

Music transmitted by word of mouth through a community, in time, develops many variants. This kind of transmission cannot produce word-for-word and note-for-note accuracy, which contrariwise – has proved to be the genre's greatest weakness, though also, its ultimate strength. Indeed, many traditional singers quite creatively and deliberately modify the material they learn. Because variants proliferate naturally, it is naive to believe that there is such a thing as the single 'authentic' version of a folksong. Despite this, by keeping such music actively alive, developing lyrics and tunes, and keeping it relevant within a community, the great tradition of folk singing has been kept alive. It is hoped the current reader enjoys this book on the subject, and is encouraged to find out more.

PREFACE

This little book contains a few old fashioned country songs. Songs which still may be heard where ploughmen strike their furrows, and still sung at harvest suppers by the old folk who do not change their tune to the times. Indeed when thus heard.... Song & Singer seem to be inseparable, for singers. such as these have a quaint personal style & an unexpected manner of prolonging their best notes which cannot be imparted & which almost baffles. notification. Nevertheless, apart from their local rendering and though these simple tunes are caged in bars, I hope that there still remains a true echo of the country in these "terrible old fashioned" songs as here presented .

Respecting their authenticity and antiquity, I will
hazard no opinion, but rather I would humbly
try to profit by the wisdom of Uncle Remus who,
it may be remembered, checked the little boy's
critical questions concerning 'Miss Meadows'
'and de gals' by telling him that 'dey wuz in dex'
'tale,—Miss Meadows en de gals wuz—'
'en de tale I give you like hi't wer? gun ter'
'me'.   .So would I preface these songs by
telling,   that — with one exception — they were
collected from the original sources above referred
to, and that anything appearing to be corrupt or
obscure either in the words or tunes is 'in de tale'
and — 'de tale I give you like hi't wer? gun'
'ter me'——— While finally I would express my
belief that the tunes & versions here given are not
included in any current British song & ballad
book .   H. S.

Brand's popular Antiquities   gives a version of the
————Wassail song but ____ no tune thereto —— —— —.

CONTENTS

THE BESOM MAKER

I am a besom maker come listen to my tale
I am a besom maker that lives in yonder vale
Sweet pleasure that I do enjoy both morning night & noon
Going o'er the hills so high O in gathering of green broom
So it's O COME BUY MY BESOMS, BESOMS FINE & NEW
BONNY GREEN BROOM BESOMS BETTER NEVER GREW

.1.

One morning as I was a roving all over the hills so high
I met the jolly squire all with his rolling eye
He tips to me the wink & I sings to him my tune
So I ease him of his drink O in gathering of green broom
So its O COME BUY etc . . . .

One morning as I was a roving until my native vale
I met Jack Sprat the miller & he asked me to turn tail
His mill I rattle round & I grind his grits so clean
So I ease him of his drink O in gathering broom so green
So it's O COME BUY etc . . . .

One morning as I was a roving until my native cot
I met a jolly farmer so happy was his lot.
He ploughed his furrows deep & he laid his corn so low
And there it would bide asleep till spring & the broom sh^d grow .
So its O COME BUY etc . . . .

And when the corn grew up upon its native soil
All like a little baby bright with its waving smile ,
Then I bundles up my broom cuts & I binds 'em tight & spare
And my besoms folks they please 'ems for I'm the darling of the
So it's O COME BUY etc . . . . (fair .

THE BESOM MAKER

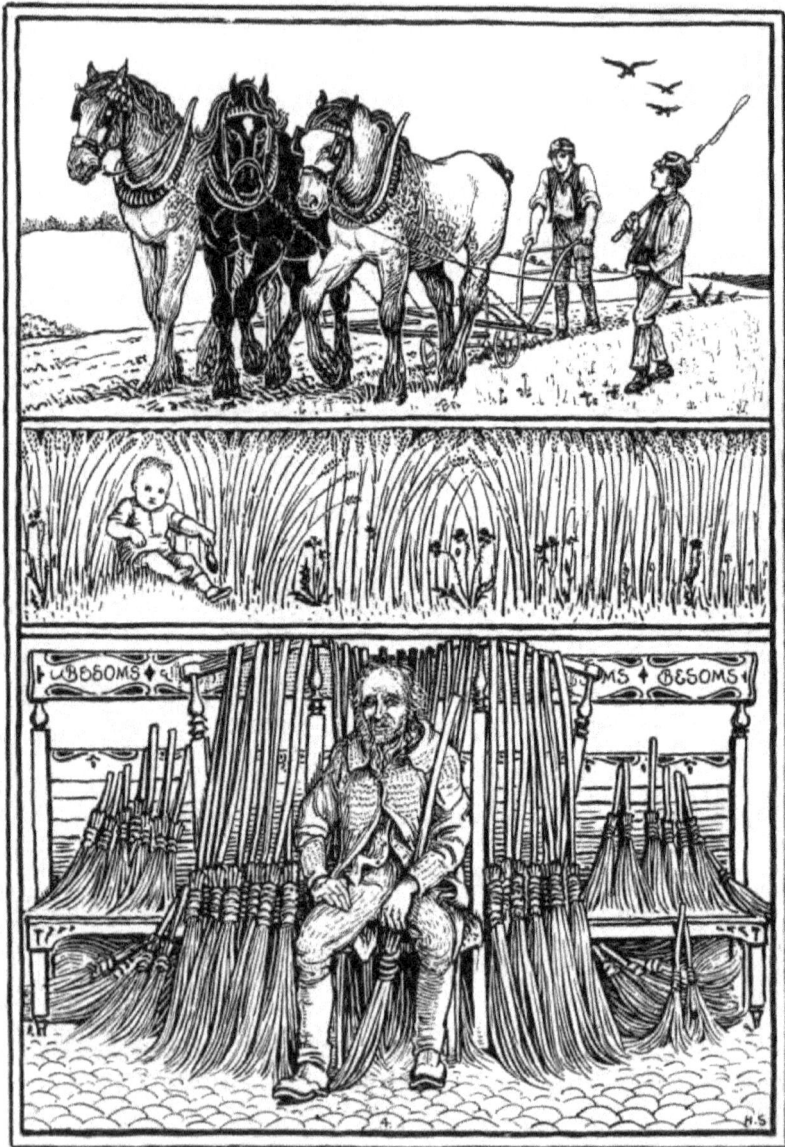

God speed the Plough

Here's a health to the farmer & God speed the plough
Send him in his fields a good crop for to grow
Send him in his fields a good crop for to grow,
That all things may prosper which he takes in hand
For the farmer indeed is a capital man.

Plough & Sow Reap & Mow
Lambs to rear & sheep to shear
Health & contentment the countrymen wear.

.5.

We build up our ricks & we fill up our barn
It's the farmer supports all the nations with corn (repeat).
Here's the blackbird & thrush we will join their sweet song
We'll be jovial together now harvest is done .
      Plough & Sow. etc.

Where young men & maidens trip over the plain
Where the sweetest of pleasures all joys do maintain (repeat)
We'll walk thro' the valleys where the valleys look gay
And the innocent lambs all around us will play .
      Plough & Sow. etc.

.6.

Now harvest is over & home we must go
Here's some to the threshing & some to the plough, (repeat)
Wi' good beef & beer we will eat dance & sing
For the farmer enjoys more his life than the king.
Plough & Sow etc

THE THE
FAR KING
MER

PETITION
Whereas...
Inasmuch
as...

8.

H.S

THE WASSAIL SONG

Pray master & mistress if you are within
Please open the door & let us come in.
For, we are come with our Christmas carol
We are come if you please to help empty your barrel.

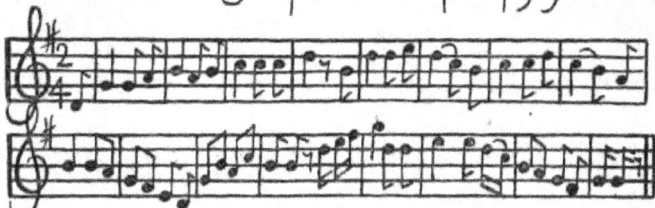

Wassail Wassail all round the town, our cup is white & our ale is brown.

CHO
RVS

Our bowl is made of a good ashen tree & here my kind fellow we drink to thee.

We are in the old Time: the new Time comes fast.
The new Time comes fast—the old Time is past.
So I wish you all a happy New Year.
Your pockets full of money, your barrels full of beer. Wassail etc

We'll drink master's health & our mistress' beside,
And all the pretty family around the fireside,
And all that he has got, I know he does not mind
We'll drink master's health in water or in wine. Wassail etc

We'll drink master's health with the star all on his breast[?]
And when that he is dead we hope his soul will rest.
So I wish you all a happy New Year
So I wish you all a happy New Year. Wassail etc.

THE WASSAIL SONG.

In western Somersetshire the chorus, as below of the Wassail song used
to be sung in apple orchards on Epiphany Eve. The observance of the
custom was supposed to bring good luck to the next year's apple crop.

Wassail Wassail all round our town.
Our cup is white, & our ale is brown.
Our bowl is made of a good ashen tree.
And here my kind fellow, we'll drink to thee.
Spoken Hats full, caps full, three bushel bags full
Apple rooms. Barns & Bartons full.
Hurrah Hurrah Hurrah. Now then once more. etc.

MY JOHNNY

My Johnny was a shoemaker & dearly he loved me
My Johnny was a shoemaker but now he's gone to sea
With nasty pitch to soil his hands
And sail across the stormy sea..ea..ea
My Johnny was a shoemaker..er..er

.11.

MY JOHNNY

His jacket was a deep sky blue & curly was his hair
His jacket was a deep sky blue it was I do declare
To reef the topsail now he's gone
And sail across the stormy sea..ea..ea
My Johnny was a shoemaker..er..er

And he will be a captain by & by with a brave & gallant crew
And he will be a captain by & by with a sword & a spy glass too
And when he is a captain bold
He'll come back to marry me..e..e
My Johnny was a shoemaker..er..er

.12.

The Reaphook &
The Sickle

Come all you lads & lasses together let us go
 Into some pleasant cornfield our courage for to show ,
With the reaphook & the sickle so well we clear the land
 The farmer says " well done my lads here's liquor at your command ".

By daylight in the morning when birds so sweetly sing
 —They are such charming creatures they make the valley ring—
We will reap & scrape together till Phœbus do go down
With the good old leathern bottle & beer that is so brown .

.13.

Lovely 🌾   Nancy 🌿

Then in comes lovely Nancy the corn all for to lay,
She is my charming creature, I must begin to pray:
See how she gathers it, binds it, she folds it in her arms,
Then gives it to some waggoner to fill a farmer's barns.

Now harvest's done & ended, the corn secure from harm,
All for to go to market boys we must thresh in the barn.
Here's a health to all you farmer's, likewise to all you men,
I wish you health & happiness till harvest comes again.

HOBBLETY BOBBLETY HOW NOW

When she churns she churns in a boot
Hobblety bobblety how now
Instead of a beater she pops in her foot
With a heigh down ho down duffle green
                                                    petticoat
Robin he thrashes her now now

———

She puts the cheese upon the shelf · Hobblety etc
And she leaves it there till it turns of itself. With etc

———

It turned of itself & went out at the door · Hobblety etc
You must make it yourself if you want any more · With etc

.15.

HOBBLETY BOBBLETY HOW NOW

She sweeps the floor but twice a year *

Hobblety Bobblety How Now

Because she says the brooms are so dear

With a heigh down ho down duffle green

petticoat

Robin he thrashes her now now

* EQVINOX?

.16.

The two young men of Kenilworth

There were 2 young men of Kenilworth the sons of 1 mother. sing
here were 2 young men of Kenilworth of Kenilworth of Kenilworth
here were 2 young men of Kenilworth
he sons of 1 Mother

ABRAHAM were the name of 1 & ISHMAEL were of t'other. sing
BRAHAM were the name of 1 the name of 1 the name of 1
BRAHAM were the name of 1
nd ISHMAEL were of t'other

These 2 young men to the field were sent the grey mare for to find. sing
hese 2 young men to the field were sent to the field were sent to the field etc
hese 2 young men to the field were sent
he grey mare for to find

ABRAHAM he got up afore and ISHMAEL sat behind. sing
BRAHAM he got up afore got up afore got up afore
BRAHAM he got up afore
nd ISHMAEL sat behind.

·17·

(To the singer — the words of each verse of this song are first said to the audience & then sung by all after the word ____ ·sing")

hese 2 young men to the play would go whenever they saw fit _ sing
hese 2 young men to the play would go to the play would go to the play
hese 2 young men to the play would go
Whenever they saw fit

BRAHAM sat in the gallery and ISHMAEL sat in the pit. sing.
BRAHAM sat in the gallery in the gallery in the gallery
BRAHAM sat in the gallery
nd ISHMAEL sat in the pit

The two young men of Kenilworth

FORTY DVKES a RIDING

19

Forty dukes a riding , my ducy dulcy officer · · · · · · · · · · ·
Forty dukes a riding , my ducy dulcy day · · · · · · · · · · · ·

What do you wish for? my ducy dulcy officer · · · · · · · · · ·
What do you wish for? my ducy dulcy day". · · · · · · · · · · ·

　　　　" I wish to catch the naughty girls naughty girls naughty girls ·
　　　　I wish to catch the naughty girls my ducy dulcy day". · ·

We are none of us naughty here sir. my ducy dulcy officer · · · · ·
We are none of us naughty here sir, my ducy dulcy day". · · · · · ·

　　　　" How do you show yr goodnels girls goodnels girls goodnels girls?
　　　　How do you show your goodness girls? my ducy dulcy day"

We all do as we are bid sir , my ducy dulcy officer · · · · · ·
We all do as we are bid sir , my ducy dulcy day". · · · · · ·

　　　　" Then I bid you to stop yr game girls game girls game girls
　　　　Then I bid you to stop yr game girls my ducy dulcy day".

.20.

We won't stop for you sir , my ducy dulcy officer· · · · · · ·
We won't stop for you sir , my ducy dulcy day"· · · · · · ·

" So naughty girls you won't obey? · ·
Then I will make you stop your play
I'll catch you one I'll catch you all
I'll catch you big I'll catch you small."

40 dukes a riding my ducy dulcy officer 40 dukes a riding my ducy dulcy day
etc·

So naughty girls you won't obey? Then I will make you stop your
play etc.

Song for the game of Blindman's Buff.

21

The Jolly Ploughboy

There were two loving brothers two brethren were born
Two brethren whose trades we still keep,
The one was a ploughman a planter of corn
The other a tender of sheep.

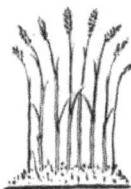

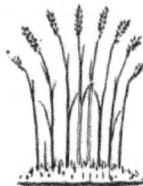

23

Come all jolly ploughboys, come help me for to sing
I'll sing in the praise of the plough.
For tho' we must labour from summer to spring
We all will be merry boys now.

We've hired we've mired thro' mire & thro' clay
No pleasure at all could we find,
Now we'll laugh dance & sing & drive care away
No more in this world to repine.

Here's April, here's May, here's June & July
Tis a pleasure to see the corn grow.
In August we moil it 'shear low & reap high
And bind up our scythes for to mow.

APRIL   MAY   JVNE & JVLY   AVGVST   H.S.

So now we have gathered up every sheaf
And scraped up every ear —
We'll make no more to do but to plough & to sow
And provide for the very next year.

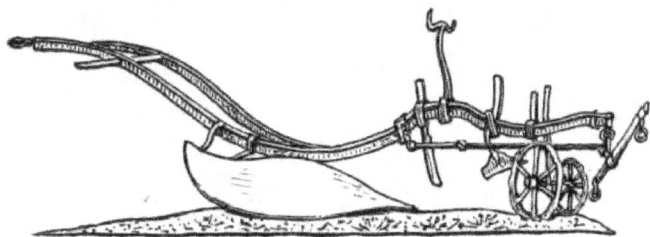

. 25 .

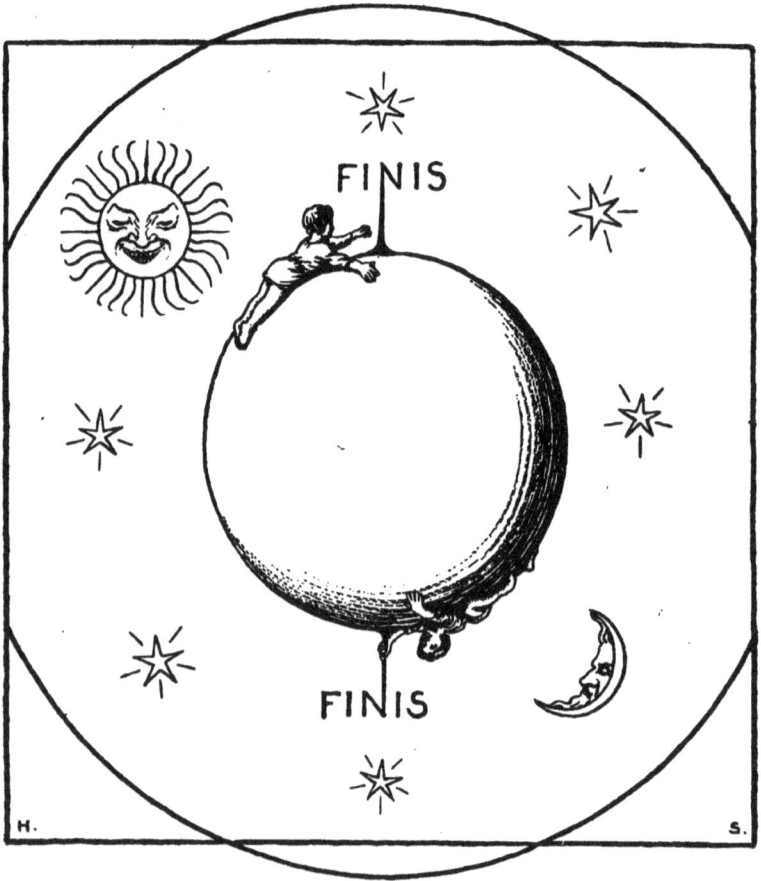

www.ingramcontent.com/pod-product-compliance
Lightning Source LLC
Chambersburg PA
CBHW021606270326
41931CB00009B/1379